Francisco Otávio Lemos da Cunha

Competence-based management:

AF154714

Francisco Otávio Lemos da Cunha

Competence-based management:

Analysis of its applicability in the merit promotion of Officers of the Santa Catarina Military Police

ScienciaScripts

This book is a translation from the original published under ISBN 978-613-9-63810-9.

Publisher:
Sciencia Scripts
is a trademark of
Dodo Books Indian Ocean Ltd. and OmniScriptum S.R.L publishing group

120 High Road, East Finchley, London, N2 9ED, United Kingdom
Str. Armeneasca 28/1, office 1, Chisinau MD-2012, Republic of Moldova, Europe
Printed at: see last page
ISBN: 978-620-7-38346-7

COMPETENCE MANAGEMENT

ANALYSIS OF THE APPLICABILITY OF MERIT-BASED PROMOTION FOR OFFICERS OF THE SANTA CATARINA MILITARY POLICE

Francisco Otavio Lemos da Cunha

Bachelor's Degree in Legal and Social Sciences from Centro Universitario Ritter dos Reis (UNIRITTER), Specialist in Integrated Public Security Management from Universidade do Sul de Santa Catarina (UNISUL) and Bachelor's Degree in Police Sciences from Academia de Policia Militar de Santa Catarina (APMT), 1st Lieutenant in the Military Police of Santa Catarina/SC, franciscotavio@hotmail.com.

Giovanni Cardoso Pacheco (Advisor)

Master in Production Engineering from the Federal University of Santa Catarina (UFSC), Specialist in Quality Management in the Public Service from the State University of Santa Catarina (UDESC), Specialist in Public Security from the University of Southern Santa Catarina (UNISUL), Specialist in Strategic Management of Public Security from the University of Vale do Itajai (UNIVALI) and Specialist in Crime Prevention from the University of Southern Santa Catarina (UNISUL), Colonel of the Military Police of Santa Catarina/SC, giopacheco67@gmail.com.

INDICE

SUMMARY

Objective: The purpose of this article is to analyze the applicability of competency-based management in the merit-based promotion of officers in the Santa Catarina Military Police (PMSC). This analysis is justified by the need to readjust the institution's performance evaluation system, making the process fairer and more up-to-date, thus achieving standards of excellence in people management that will have a direct impact on organizational results.

Design/Methodology/Approach: The research was carried out using the deductive method, with bibliographic and exploratory research as the research technique. This methodology allowed the researcher to compare how merit-based promotions of PMSC officers are currently processed, with the guidelines of competency-based management and current performance evaluation systems.

Results: It was concluded that competency-based management is perfectly applicable to the dictates that guide the merit promotion of Officers, as it is reconciled with the principles of hierarchy and discipline that govern military institutions. However, its application within the PMSC requires a thorough overhaul of its performance evaluation criteria, as well as its processing system.

Originality/value: The PMSC's top managers are the Officers and it is through them that the institution makes its strategic decisions in order to directly interfere in the provision of services to society. This article provides a current view of competency-based people management as a way of achieving excellent institutional results.

Keywords: promotion. merit. management. competencies. evaluation.

COMPETENCY MANAGEMENT

ANALYSIS OF THE APPLICABILITY IN THE PROMOTION BY MERIT OF OFFICERS OF THE MILITARY POLICE OF SANTA CATARINA

ABSTRACT

Goal: This article aims to analyze the applicability of competency management in the merit promotion of officers of the Military Police of Santa Catarina (PMSC). This analysis is justified by the need to re-adjust to the institution's performance evaluation system, making the process more fair and current, thus achieving standards of excellence in people management that will directly impact organizational results.

Design/ Methodology/ Approach: The research was developed using the deductive method, having as research technique the bibliographic and exploratory. This methodology allowed the researcher to compare how the merit promotions of PMSC Officers are currently being processed, with the guidelines of competency management and current performance evaluation systematic.

Results: It was concluded that competency-based management is perfectly applicable to the dictates that guide the merit promotion of Officers, because it reconciles with the principles of hierarchy and discipline that govern military institutions. However, the application under the PMSC needs a deep reformulation in its performance evaluation criteria, as well as in its processing systematic.

Originality / value: The great managers of the PMSC are the Officers and through them the institution makes its strategic decisions in a way that directly interferes with the provision of services to society. This article presents a current vision about the management of people by competences as a way to achieve institutional results of excellence.

Keywords: promotion. merit. management. competences. evaluation.

---

1   INTRODUCTION

The Santa Catarina Military Police (PMSC) has challenging objectives set out in its Strategic Plan. One of its aspirations is to be recognized as an institution that provides excellent services and, in order to achieve this goal, one of the corporation's strategic dimensions is human and organizational capital (SANTA CATARINA, 2015). This article stems from this strategic objective of the institution, coupled with the need to reformulate people management in order to promote the continuous personal and professional improvement of its officers, making them more motivated and committed to the pursuit of excellent results.

The subject of people management is challenging and extremely complex for any organization and its correct management can be the differential for maximizing results. Thus, considering that competency-based management is a current issue in the business sector and is used in large organizations that stand out in their field, this study is relevant because it shows how competency-based management can be reconciled with the principles that govern a military institution and the results that can come from implementing this management model.

The research was carried out using the deductive method, with bibliographic and exploratory research as the research technique. The analysis of competency-based management in the Santa Catarina Military Police aims to demonstrate the possibility of its application in the merit promotion criteria for officers.

To this end, theoretical research will be carried out on the foundations of competency-based management, explaining its aims and advantages for the organization, as well as describing the way in which merit-based promotions of officers are currently carried out.

Finally, some considerations will be presented regarding the reformulation of the promotion criteria and system in order to make it possible to adapt its processing to the competency-based management guidelines.

2   DEVELOPMENT

2.1 Competency-based management

The analysis of competency-based management requires a correct understanding and consequent differentiation between management and people management, until finally arriving at competency-based management, the central object of this study.

Management, according to the Michaelis dictionary (2014), consists of "the act of managing, administering and running a particular business". In this case, it is the "management competency" in which the organization can be based on one or more organizational models (RESENDE, 2003). Therefore, it can be inferred that the term management is very broad, from which certain concepts and management models are derived that affect any organization.

One of the most important points for any public or private institution is people, since "they are fundamental parts of organizations, and interfere directly in the organizational structure" (MACHADO; MELCHERT; MAKUFKA, 2011, p. 186). The need to pay special attention to the people who make up an organization is based on the fact that they are considered to be the main element for managers to invest in, since the guarantee of organizational results lies in obtaining qualified and motivated professionals (LAPOLLI; SILVA; SANTO, 2009).

It should be noted that each and every organization is made up of people and depends on them to achieve its objectives and fulfill its missions (CHIAVENATO, 2010). In this sense, "intellectual capital, which are the intangible assets of organizations, are the most valuable assets in this knowledge society" (MACHADO; MELCHERT; MAKUFKA, 2011, p. 190).

Therefore, the success of a company depends more and more on the people who make up its staff, since they contribute through their ideas, skills, experience and work to achieve the objectives and goals of an organization (MACHADO; MELCHERT; MAKUFKA, 2011). Therefore, people management is the tool that helps managers carry out their functions (planning, organizing, directing and controlling) through the people who make up their team (CHIAVENATO, 2010).

When dealing with people management, Chiavenato (2010, p. 8) states:

> People management (PM) is an area that is very sensitive to the mentality that prevails in organizations. It is extremely contingent and situational, as it depends on various aspects, such as the culture that exists in each organization, the organizational structure adopted, the characteristics of the environmental context, the organization's business, the technology used, the internal processes, the management style used and a multitude of other important variables.

In turn, the objectives of people management are varied and contribute to organizational effectiveness through the following means: They help the organization achieve its objectives and accomplish its mission; they provide the organization with competitiveness; they provide the organization with well-trained and well-motivated people; they increase people's self-actualization and satisfaction at work; they develop and maintain quality of life at work; they manage and drive change; they maintain ethical policies and socially responsible behavior and aim to build the best company and the best team (CHIAVENATO, 2010).

When approaching the subject of people management, it is worth highlighting its basic processes, as described by Chiavenato (2010): the process of adding people, the process of applying people, the process of rewarding people, the process of developing people, the process of keeping people and the process of monitoring people. These people management processes are complex and need to interact with each other in such a way that one does not harm the other and together they increase organizational results.

One way of integrating these processes in a balanced way is through the use of a balanced scorecard (CHIAVENATO, 2010). This methodology "translates the mission and strategy of organizations into a balanced and comprehensive set of performance measures, which serve as the basis for a measurement and strategic management system." (ANDRADE; AMBONI, 2010, p. 74).

Managing people consists of "achieving a high degree of cooperation and commitment, and this is more than managing people, it is managing with people" (CHIAVENATO, 2005, 313). In order to achieve the levels of excellence sought in its strategic planning, an organization needs people and their correct management is the crucial point for this aspiration.

Given this reality and the importance of applying the best way of managing people, competency-based management was born. According to Dessler (2003 apud GIRARDI et al., 2009, p. 39) "competence is related to characteristics such as knowledge, skills and behaviors that enable performance."

In line with this idea, it follows that:

> Competence management deals with the establishment and continuous development of competences, helping Knowledge Management to create knowledge through creativity, flexibility and so on (GIRARDI et al., 2009, p. 39).

Qualified people, working in the right roles, on the one hand bring countless benefits and increase the profitability of organizations, and on the other make people happy and fulfilled in what they do (MACHADO; MELCHERT; MAKUFKA, 2011). For this reason, competency-based people management is of the utmost importance, as it prevents the loss of talent or the underutilization of a qualified workforce that the organization has at its disposal, creating a favourable working environment where people are happy and satisfied.

Management by competencies as taught by Resende (2003, p. 152) "means implementing plans with the application of management principles and techniques to develop specific competencies that executives, teams or areas need to acquire and apply."

Competence can be understood in two dimensions according to Ruano (2003, p. 22):

> [...] the strategic (corporate) and the individual. The first deals with organizational competencies and refers to the company as a whole. The second deals with the competence of the people who work in the organization. Although conceptually there is a distinction between the dimensions, in the performance of organizational practice they are closely linked.

Personal competencies can be summed up as the set of technical and behavioral competencies that a professional possesses, made up of the triad (knowledge, skills and attitudes), i.e. knowing, knowing how to do and wanting to do (RABAGLIO, 2001). In this context, Resende (2003, p. 153) states that "where the concept and model of competence are having more innovative and specific applications is in human resource management. And it's only natural, because at the end of the day, even technical and organizational competencies are underpinned by personal competencies."

Competence, as has been shown, has a double bias: the organizational and the individual. It should be noted that the two are totally related, and it is not possible to establish individual competencies without first reflecting on organizational competencies, i.e. organizations cannot live without the *expertise of* people and people, in turn, cannot live without the *expertise of* organizations (RUANO, 2003).

This understanding gives rise to the term "core *competences",* which are considered to be "a set of skills and technologies that result in providing a fundamental differential for a company's competitiveness" (RUANO, 2003, p. 22-23).

Since core competencies deal with competencies from a broader perspective, i.e. the corporate perspective, they must be diagnosed in two stages, the first analyzing business competencies and the second human competencies (RUANO, 2003).

In the light of this, the question arises as to why the competency-based management model should be applied in organizations. There are several answers, the main ones being the search for excellent management standards, the identification and development of strategic competencies, stimulating the self-development of the qualifications and skills of managers and all employees, the management and retention of talent, the management of careers and the search for fairer and more transparent remuneration criteria (RESENDE, 2003).

Management by competencies interferes in various areas of the institution and has a broad application, as Resende (2002, p. 20) teaches:

> Definition of the company's core competencies, in order to focus efforts on the points that will enable it to improve performance standards and conditions of excellence more quickly.
> Definition of managerial competencies, with the aim of giving more objectivity to management training and development plans. Identifying job competencies to serve as a benchmark for differentiating basic salaries, selection, training and staff movements.
> Competency-based career modules or stages. It is the model of the plan or system that we have developed in various companies.

Therefore, competency-based management seeks to reconcile organizational competency with the competencies of the people who are part of the institution and there are various ways of doing this. Reis (2003, p. 10) teaches that the "advantage of working with the concept of competence is that it allows the focus to be directed, concentrating energies on what needs to be worked on in order for the company to achieve its operational and strategic objectives."

Remuneration and career is a point that deserves to be highlighted due to the gains that the institution can obtain with the correct application of competency-based management in this area. Resende (2003) mentions that the use of traditional practices characterized by weak policies and unobjective career and remuneration criteria cause various problems for organizations, such as job dissatisfaction, low productivity and quality, vulnerability to lawsuits, wasted salary funds and the loss of good employees.

In this area, the advances that can be brought about by reformulating the management of the job and salary plan through management based on competencies and skills tend to minimize the weakest points in order to have a more professional management with a sense of consequence, with fairer and more transparent criteria, with firmer and more consistent management policies, always remembering the importance of *feedback* (RESENDE, 2002).

The need to make proper use of the skills of the company's existing staff requires proper career management in order to keep talent by developing their potential, investing in staff more objectively, treating them more appropriately and maximizing the use of their knowledge and skills (RESENDE, 2002).

Career development should be carried out using transparent and fair criteria in order to avoid employee dissatisfaction by creating and using "instruments such as the job profile with indications of the requirements demanded of its occupants, and the evaluation of the potential of the people considered for promotion." (RESENDE, 2002, p. 27).

The purpose of the competency-based approach to people management in this topic was to demonstrate its basic concepts and how it influences the organization when it is implemented. The main focus was on the career and the correct use of the competencies of the staff, given that this is the object of analysis of this study in relation to the reality of the Santa Catarina Military Police.

2.2 Systematic merit promotion of PMSC officers

The use of competency-based people management adds fundamental and indispensable qualities to any organization. This is no different in a military institution, which needs results as a way of acquiring and maintaining its legitimacy arising from the trust placed in it by society. These excellent results will only be achieved through the continuous training and motivation of its staff.

One of the ways to promote this search for professional training and to increase motivation for the work of an organization's staff is the expectation of career advancement. Currently, in the PMSC, there are various ways of promoting officers, which will be carried out according to the following criteria, as established in art. 62 of Law No. 6.218/83: merit, seniority, bravery, "post-mortem", intellectual merit and required, with automatic transfer to the paid reserve (SANTA CATARINA, 1983c).

This section will analyze the way in which the promotion for merit (merecimento) of the Officers of the Santa Catarina Military Police is currently carried out. The concept of merit promotion is laid down in §1 of art. 62 of Law 6.218/83, which reads as follows:

> A merit-based promotion is one based on a set of attributes and

qualities that distinguish and enhance the value of a soldier among his peers, assessed during the course of his career and in the performance of positions, commissions and duties, particularly in the rank or grade he holds, when he is listed and nominated for promotion (SANTA CATARINA, 1983c).

This concept should not be confused with intellectual merit, which is provided for in §7 of art. 62 of the aforementioned law: "Promotion for intellectual merit is that which occurs after completion of a training course or competition and is based on the final numerical concept, observing the descending order and the number of vacancies" (SANTA CATARINA, 1983c).

It can be seen from the concept of merit promotion that for an officer to be promoted, an analysis is made of the attributes and qualities that distinguish him and enhance his values, in other words, a measurement of the personal skills that this officer possesses and has demonstrated throughout his career. It should be noted that the assessment is based on past skills and performance without, however, measuring whether the officer is prepared to take on a role that requires new professional and personal skills different from those already practiced.

In addition, for promotion by merit, the officer must meet certain requirements to be included in the access list, which are divided into access conditions (interstice, physical aptitude and peculiarities of each rank in the different cadres), professional concept and moral concept (SANTA CATARINA, 1983b).

Officers' professional and moral standing will be assessed by the Military Police Officers' Promotion Commission (CPOPM) by examining the promotion documentation and other information received. The aforementioned concepts are assessed through the Information Sheets in a single copy. These are confidential in nature and not even the officer who has received the award can have access to the information on the form (SANTA CATARINA,

1983a).

The forms are filled out once a semester and may contain comments that must be made by June 30 and December 31, and sent to the CPOPM within 10 days of the end of the semester. When the grade given on the form is insufficient (less than or equal to 2.00) or exceptional (equal to or greater than 5.01), the issuing officer must justify it (SANTA CATARINA, 1983a).

In turn, the access framework is defined, according to art. 27, § 2 of Law 6.215/83, as being:

> § Paragraph 2 and the list of Officers eligible for access is the result of an assessment of the merit and quality required for promotion, which must take into account, in addition to other requirements
> I - efficiency in the performance of positions and commissions, not their intrinsic nature or the length of time they have been held;
> II - the potential for higher positions;
> III - leadership skills, initiative and quick decision-making;
> IV - the results of the regulatory courses held;
> V - the Officer's prominence among his peers (SANTA CATARINA, 1983b).

The merit promotion boards are processed and organized by the CPOPM, and "the work of this body involving the merit assessment of a PM officer and the respective documentation will be classified as confidential" (SANTA CATARINA, 1983b). It is important to note that the CPOPM does not only process merit promotions, but all types of officer promotion.

The CPOPM is set up in accordance with Article 26 of Law 6.215/83, which reads as follows:

> Art. 26: The PM Officers' Promotion Commission is permanent, made up of natural and permanent members and chaired by the General Commander of the Corporation.

§ Paragraph 1 - The Chief of Staff and the Director of Personnel of the Corporation are natural born members.

§ Paragraph 2 - Half of the ready Colonels of the Military Police and four (4) more Senior Military Police Officers, who are replaced annually, shall be effective members.

§ Paragraph 3: When filling vacancies for the rank of Colonel, the Commission for the Promotion of Military Officers (CPOPM) will be made up exclusively of all the ready-made Colonels of the Military Police.

§ Paragraph 4 - The CPOPM will be secretariat by a senior officer appointed by the Commanding General.

§ Paragraph 5 - The regulations of this Law will define the duties and operation of the CPOPM (SANTA CATARINA, 1983b).

In order to be eligible for inclusion in the Access Board by merit, the officer must be considered to have "sufficient" merit in the CPOPM's judgment, according to article 16 of State Decree 19.236/83 (SANTA CATARINA, 1983a). In addition, the aforementioned State Decree states in its article 26 that the CPOPM's judgment of the officer for the purposes of inclusion in the access cadre will take into account:

I - the assessments contained in the Information Sheets;

II - the efficiency revealed in the performance of positions and commissions, particularly the performance in the position in question, in command, leadership or direction;

III - the potential for higher positions;

IV - leadership skills, initiative and quick decision-making;

V - the results obtained in regulatory courses;

VI - the spotlight among their peers;

VII - the punishments suffered in his post;

VIII - serving a custodial sentence at the post, or suspension from exercising the office or function inherent to the post;

IX - leave of absence to attend to private interests. Sole Paragraph -

> The final judgment of the PM Officer considered not qualified for access, on a provisional basis, must be justified, entered in the minutes and submitted to the General Commander of the Corporation (SANTA CATARINA, 1983a).

Article 27 of the State Decree under study states that in addition to the factors mentioned above, the following are considered for entry into the Merit-based Access Ranks: concepts, mentions, length of service, injuries in action, work deemed useful and approved by the institution's competent body, national medals and decorations, commendable references, outstanding achievements and other activities considered meritorious by the corporation (SANTA CATARINA, 1983a).

Likewise, factors that are indicative of demerit, such as punishments, convictions or failure to complete courses as an officer, will be taken into account for the purposes of issuing the concept, as provided for in art. 28. It should also be noted that in the case of merit-based promotions, the Governor of the State will freely assess the merit of the officers included in the proposal submitted by the Commanding General (SANTA CATARINA, 1983a).

The importance of promotion by merit in the career of officers can be seen in the provisions of art. 10 of Law 6.215/83, which establishes how promotions will be made. This regulation states that promotion to 2nd lieutenant will take place in 01 (one) vacancy by seniority and 01 (one) by merit, with regard to promotion to 1st lieutenant there will be 01 (one) by seniority and 02 (two) by merit, for Captain there will be 01 (one) by seniority and 03 (three) by merit and finally for Major, Lieutenant Colonel and Colonel all by merit (SANTA CATARINA, 1983b).

The aforementioned article strongly emphasizes the importance of merit-based promotion for officers' careers, since an officer can only become a senior officer (major, lieutenant colonel and colonel) through merit. And to make the CPOPM's evaluation of merit even more important, art. 31 of Law

6.215/83 states that:

> Art. 31 Officers who fail to appear three times, consecutively or not, on a merit-based access board, if a more modern officer participated in each one, shall be considered ineligible for promotion to the next rank on the merit-based criterion.
>
> Paragraph 1: A lieutenant-cellar who appears at the head of the list three (3) consecutive times for promotion on merit may not be passed over (SANTA CATARINA, 1983b).

It is clear from this article that if an officer does not appear on the Merit Access List for three (3) consecutive times or not, and appears with the same more modern officer, he will be considered ineligible for promotion to the next rank on the merit criterion. It is worth noting that it is not enough for an officer to appear on the merit-based access board, but that he must have a favorable concept in order to be among the top ranks with the aim of being promoted. This is clear from the provisions of articles 49 and 50 of State Decree 19.236/83:

> Art.49 - Promotion by merit, up to and including the rank of PM lieutenant colonel, will be based on the Access Board by merit, according to the following criteria:
>
> I - for the first vacancy, one of the two PM Officers occupying the top two positions on the Access List will be selected;
>
> II - for the second vacancy, a PM officer will be selected from the remainder of the contenders for the first vacancy, plus the two immediately following;
>
> III - for the third vacancy, a PM officer will be selected from the remainder of the contestants for the second vacancy, plus the two immediately following, and so on.
>
> Sole paragraph - No reduction may occur in the number of merit-

based promotions as a result of the respective Access Board having a number of PM Officers less than twice the number of vacancies provided for by the merit-based criterion (SANTA CATARINA, 1983a).

He adds:

> Art. 50 - Promotion by merit to the rank of PM Colonel will be made on the basis of the Access Board by merit, according to the following criteria:
> I - for the first vacancy, one of the first five lieutenant colonels will be selected from among those eligible for promotion and listed in the QAM;
> II - for the other vacancies, the provisions of items II and III will be complied with.
> III from the previous article (SANTA CATARINA, 1983a).

The arithmetic mean of the values assigned in the Officers' information sheets for the same rank will constitute the rank concept grade. Article 32 of the aforementioned State Decree stipulates that this arithmetic average of values will be assigned individually by the members of the committee, with values ranging from 01 (one) to 06 (six). These are considered to be Excellent (5.01 to 6.00), Very Good (4.01 to 5.00), Good (3.01 to 4.00), Fair (2.01 to 3.00) and Insufficient (1.00 to 2.00) (SANTA CATARINA, 1983a).

The promotion form will be made up of the algebraic sum of the rank concept, the objective criteria set out in articles 27 and 28 of State Decree 19.236/83 and the numerical value obtained as a result of the CPOPM judgment, establishing the total points and classifying the officer in the merit access table (SANTA CATARINA, 1983a).

It should be noted that the information sheet to be filled in by the

CPOPM has eminently subjective criteria that have a great deal of weight in assigning total points and classifying the officer in the respective Access Board. This is the crucial point that deserves to be highlighted and analyzed in detail in order to indicate a new format for the merit promotion of officers.

2.3 Competency-based management in the merit promotion of PMSC officers

The precepts inherent in competency-based management are applicable in the area of personnel management, especially with regard to career promotion. The purpose of this topic is to indicate an adjustment in the way the merit-based promotion of officers is processed, with the aim of maintaining the basic principles of military institutions, increasing institutional power and reducing the occurrence of distortions that can be a determining factor in the performance of excellent service and even the retention of talent.

As we have seen, competency-based management brings numerous benefits to the institution and its employees. These guidelines can and should be applied in institutions that aspire to provide excellent services and leverage their results.

The Santa Catarina Military Police is no different and can use the practice of competency-based management to become a more competitive, legitimate institution with sustainable results, without giving up its institutional foundations: hierarchy and discipline. This concern is demonstrated in the PMSC's 2013/2014 Command Plan, which aims, among other things, to be recognized by society as a legitimate, effective institution that provides excellent services (SANTA CATARINA, 2013).

In this vein, Chiavenato (2005, p. 7) states that "knowing how to achieve competitiveness depends not only on winning, retaining, applying, developing, motivating and rewarding talent, but mainly on managing skills and achieving significant results through them". As has been shown, the Santa Catarina Military Police is aware of this factor and knows that only through favorable working conditions and a solid career will it achieve the desired goals.

Based on these objectives, the Command Plan has as one of its two major areas of concern the "MILITARY POLICEMEN" and, inserted in this optic, is the promotion of Officers, which is thus set as a goal to be achieved: "ensure that Officers are promoted based on objectively measured criteria and based on functional performance, institutional values and academic and technical-professional knowledge." (SANTA CATARINA, 2013, p. 25). It should be noted that the promotion of Officers takes place in the so-called vertical career, which Resende (2002, p. 30-31) explains "professionals are promoted to hierarchically superior positions, which implies changes in the nature and level of responsibilities of the positions, if they meet the qualification and experience requirements." And he adds: "[...] As a reward they receive the salary of the new position."

Remuneration has a direct impact on careers, given the salary increase for promoted officers. Furthermore, with regard to remuneration, the Command Plan establishes the goal of carrying out "ongoing support to promote professional development through remuneration commensurate with the importance of military police work" (SANTA CATARINA, 2013, p. 25).

At this point, it is necessary to go into the criteria for measuring and evaluating performance, which can be defined as a:

> systematic assessment of each person's performance, based on the activities they perform, the goals and results to be achieved, the skills they offer and their development potential (CHIAVENATO, 2010, p. 241).

From this concept, it can be seen that performance appraisals serve not only as a measurement criterion for promotion, but also as *feedback* on the professional's performance, with a view to continuous improvement and the services provided by the institution. An analysis of the way in which PMSC officers are promoted on merit shows that the corporation currently uses two main criteria for evaluation: objective and subjective. The first are closed criteria, because the person being evaluated either meets the requirements or they don't, leaving subjectivity to one side.

In the case of the PMSC, the objective criteria are clear and cover the peculiarities of a military organization, measuring medals, decorations, courses taken and completed by the Officer as well as their intellectual development such as graduation, post-graduation, masters, doctorate. However, one factor that could be added to the current objective measurement criteria for promotion would be the use of the PMSC's innovative management tool: *"BI"*.

BI is a *business intelligence* tool that "aims to support the decision-making process" (SANTA CATARINA, 2013, p. 30). Nowadays, this modern system is more than just a support system for decision-making, it is a tool for measuring the results of the most diverse areas of the PMSC, supporting changes in behavior to achieve excellent results or even the achievement of indices considered competitive by the institution.

The use of "BI" in a more focused, responsible and even serious way requires a continuous process of acculturation of the officers, who are the institution's main managers. One way of raising this awareness is to use it as an objective criterion to be scored and measured for promotion on merit.

One point worth highlighting is that the laws that deal with the merit-based promotion of officers in the Santa Catarina Military Police are too old and must be adapted to the new reality that the police are experiencing. The evaluation is currently carried out only by the officer's commander and the CPOPM. This evaluation can lead to dysfunctions that do not demonstrate the officer's real competence, and the officer may be disadvantaged at some point.

One possibility, widely disseminated by authors in the field of administration, to carry out the performance evaluation in order to avoid and/or minimize these possible distortions would be to extend it beyond the commander and CPOPM, but also to the peers who work directly with him, and even to his subordinates. This method of performance appraisal is called 360° appraisal, which consists of a circular appraisal carried out by all those who interact with the appraisee in some way (CHIAVENATO, 2010).

According to Chiavenato (2010, p. 246):

> The assessment made by the environment is richer because it produces different information from all sides and works to ensure the employee's adaptability and adjustment to the various demands they receive from their work environment or their partners.

The use of the 360° appraisal would tend to reduce some of the dysfunction of the officer's appraisal by taking a holistic view. For example, an officer who doesn't discipline his troops or is sloppy with his duties could have a more beneficial evaluation from his subordinates, but on the other hand, the evaluation from his commander, peers and CPOPM would tend to be negative, because the person being evaluated fails in this aspect, which is one of his duties.

Another option is the so-called self-assessment, which "is a process in which the person being assessed analyzes their own performance using the same assessment factors or performance indicators" (CHIAVENATO, 2005, p. 254). In other words, it would be one more factor to be assessed when formulating the Officer's final concept.

Now, the way in which officer promotions are currently carried out is widely criticized, since the measurement is carried out by a performance evaluation committee, according to Chiavenato (2010, p. 247), "despite the obvious distribution of forces, this alternative is widely criticized for its strongly centralizing aspect and its spirit of judgment about the past". He adds: "[...] For this reason, it is difficult for the central committee to focus on guiding and continuously improving performance." However, it should be stressed that the evaluation carried out by the CPOPM is essential, especially in a military organization with deeply-rooted values.

In turn, it should be noted that the 360° performance evaluation is complex and must be very well disseminated within the organization and aligned with the program's strategic mission. Furthermore, the competencies covered in the form must be aligned with the institution's objectives and must not be so broad as to make it impossible to link them to the appraisee's individual performance (SNELL; BOHLANDER, 2010).

360° evaluation is widespread in business, especially in successful companies. Snell and Bohlander (2010, p. 308) explain that "[...] more than 90% of the companies named among Fortune magazine's 1,000 have implemented some form of 360-degree *feedback* system for career development, performance evaluation or both".

A multi-factor evaluation tends to reduce distortions that may appear consciously or unconsciously on the part of the evaluator. These judgment biases are explained as follows:

> 1. Consciously: when the evaluator under any pretext "biases" a result, intentionally premeditating to serve interests at stake or seeking to help or harm the evaluee.
> 2. Unconsciously: When the evaluator takes the same actions as before, but without the premeditated, malicious intention of causing a change in the original result (MARRAS, 2011, p. 171).

Another adaptation that needs to be rethought is that nowadays the concept given to Officers through the evaluation form is confidential. This prevents the appraisee from getting *feedback* on their work *performance so that they* can reflect on the improvements they need to make in order to boost their performance in the next appraisal. In this sense, Snell and Bohlander (2010, p. 300) teach that "[...] appraisals provide essential *feedback* to discuss employees' strengths and weaknesses and also to improve performance".

With regard to the assessment criteria, it would also be necessary to rethink the competencies to be assessed in order to adapt them to the current reality of the officers. It is necessary to formulate different evaluation forms for each post held, as the responsibilities are different and so are the skills expected of the person being evaluated.

The application must also be differentiated with regard to the middle and operational areas due to the peculiarities of each of them and the service performed by the Officer. With this in mind, Lucena (1999, p. 101) explains:

> The structuring and description of positions are stages in organizational planning that seek, based on the mission and areas of responsibility of each organizational unit, to establish the work positions, their duties, responsibilities and authorities. Job descriptions also specify the scope of each position, the expected contribution and the professional and personal skills required to perform the job.

At this point, the possibility of adapting the merit-based promotion of Military Police Officers to the dictates of competency-based management becomes clear, since each rank requires different conduct and competencies. And for each activity carried out, whether in the middle or operational areas, it is necessary to establish different measurement criteria.

As has been shown, it is not enough to simply adapt the assessment method; the correct development of subjective assessment factors is crucial for the corporation and its officers. Chiavenato (2005, p. 263) explains this issue thus:

> Recent research has shown a positive correlation between successful companies and the presence of performance evaluation procedures for their staff. These successful companies are more focused on performance appraisal systems centered on results achieved based on expectations previously negotiated and established between appraiser and appraisee than on the personal characteristics of the appraisee.

Furthermore, these dictates must be based on the principle of publicity. In which the factors are well disseminated and known to all, the Officer being evaluated is aware of the skills that are expected and even which of them must be developed.

A contrasting point in the merit evaluation of PMSC officers is the possibility that the officer with the best concept may not be promoted. This is due to the provision that the decision to choose is made by the Governor of the State through the list sent by the CPOPM. This provision should have been adapted in the sense that the Governor would authorize the vacancies for promotion, but the decision would be taken by the institution after the process of determining the concept has been completed, and the promotions would be made on merit in the order determined by the PMSC Commander General.

3   FINAL CONSIDERATIONS

Competency-based management is a current and widespread topic in the business sector. Its applicability is complex and requires significant changes in organizational trends and practices, especially in a military institution. However, it is a viable alternative for achieving excellent organizational and personal results.

The first part of the study aimed to explain what competency-based management is, its purposes and advantages for the organization, as well as the complexity involved in its application. The second part was a legal survey of how merit-based promotions of PMSC officers are currently processed, pointing out their peculiarities and most sensitive topics.

Finally, some alternatives were presented for reformulating the promotion criteria and system in order to make it possible to adapt their processing to the competency-based management guidelines. It was also shown that competency-based management is flexible and can be adapted to any sector, including the military. It also has the ability to add results of excellence to the organization, which consequently reflects in the provision of its services to society.

Analyzing the feasibility of applying competency-based management to the merit-based promotion of officers in the Santa Catarina Military Police proves to be an effective alternative for reformulating the promotion process for officers, making the criteria fairer and more widely known. Such a measure would avoid distortions that could curtail the professional's career or even cause discontent that would affect their performance and interfere with the institution's results. It would also reduce the risk of losing talented officers.

It is concluded that the merit-based promotion of officers should be reformulated and can be based on the dictates of competency-based management in order to achieve excellent results in the provision of services to society. The analysis carried out shows that, in order to adapt to competency-based management, the Officer merit promotion process needs to be thoroughly studied in terms of the criteria to be measured in order to form the Officer's concept. Evaluations should be based on well-defined competencies according to the post to be held and differentiating between operational and administrative areas.

It is necessary to adapt the system in order to make the evaluation broader and fairer, with the aim of providing *feedback and* fostering the officer's continuous improvement process. Another point worth highlighting is the inclusion of "BI" results in the performance evaluation criteria, in order to maximize the use of this tool.

ANNEXI

LAW NO. 6.215, OF FEBRUARY 10, 1983

Origin: Government

Nature: PL 14/83

DO: 12.153 of 11/02/83

Partially amended by Laws: 6.703/85; LC 130/94; 13.569/05

See LC 370/07

Partially repealed by LC 130/94

Regulation Decrees: 19.236-(14/03/83); 3676-(9/11/05)

NOTE: Decree: 19.236-(14/03/83) was amended by Decrees: 22758-(24/04/84); 22105-(29/05/84); 24516-(21/12/84); 31729-(12/03/87); 1477-(6/04/88); 926-(05/12/07); 801-(12/04/96); 216-(13/07/95); 729-(20/10/07); 153-(24/05/95)

Source: ALESC/Div. Documentation

Provides for the Promotion of State Military Police Officers, and other measures.

THE GOVERNOR OF THE STATE OF SANTA CATARINA,

I hereby inform all the inhabitants of this state that the Legislative Assembly has enacted and I hereby sanction the following law:

CHAPTER I

GENERALITIES

Art. 1 This law establishes the criteria and conditions that ensure that officers in the active ranks of the Santa Catarina State Military Police have access to the military-police hierarchy by means of selective, gradual and successive promotion.

Art. 2 Promotion is an administrative act and its basic purpose is the selective filling of vacancies at the higher hierarchical level, on the basis of the staffing levels established by law, for the different cadres.

Art. 3 The gradual and successive form will result from career planning for military police officers, organized in the MP.

Paragraph one. The planning thus carried out shall ensure a regular and balanced career flow.

CHAPTER II

PROMOTION CRITERIA

Art. 4 Promotions shall be made on the basis of :

a) - seniority;

b) - merit;

c) - for bravery;

d) - "post-mortem".

Sole paragraph. In extraordinary cases, there may be a promotion to compensate for the loss.

Art. 5 Promotion by seniority is based on the hierarchical precedence of an OM officer over others of equal rank within the same cadre.

Art. 6 - Promotion by merit is based on the set of attributes and qualities that distinguish and enhance the value of the PM Officer among his peers, assessed during his career and in the performance of the positions and commissions he holds in particular, when he is considered for promotion.

Art. 7: The promotion for bravery is the one that results from an act or acts of courage and audacity, which go beyond the normal limits of the fulfillment of duty and represent indispensable or useful deeds in police-military operations, due to the results achieved or the positive example they set.

Art. 8: "Post-mortem" promotion is that which aims to express the State's recognition of the PM Officer who died in the line of duty or as a result of it, or to recognize the right of the PM Officer to whom the promotion was due, unenforced due to death.

Art. 9 - Promotion in compensation for reprieve is made after the PM Officer who was reprieved has been recognized as entitled to the promotion that would have been his.

Sole paragraph. The promotion referred to in this article will be carried out according to the criteria of seniority or merit, with the PM Officer receiving the number he was entitled to in the hierarchical scale, as if he had been promoted at the appropriate time, without any modification to previous acts.

Art. 10: Promotions are made:

a) for 2nd lieutenant PM vacancies, by seniority criterion;

b) for the vacancies of Lieutenant PM, Captain PM, Major PM and Lieutenant Colonel PM, by the criteria of seniority and merit, according to the proportionality between them established in the regulations of this Law;

c) for the vacancies of Colonel PM only by the criterion of merit.

Sole paragraph. When a PM Officer applies for promotion on both criteria, the seniority vacancy may be filled on the merit criterion, without prejudice to the calculation of future merit quotas.

LC N° 130/94 (Art.3) - (DO. 15.054 of 16/11/94)

Article 10 ... of Law No. 6.215, of February 10, 1983, shall read as follows:

"Art. 10 Promotions will be made, in the respective cadres, in accordance with the number of vacancies, as follows:

I - to 2nd Lieutenant, 01 (one) by seniority and 01 (one) by merit;

II - to 1st Lieutenant, one (01) by seniority and two (02) by merit;

III - to Captain, 01 (one) by seniority and 03 (three) by merit;

IV - Major, Lieutenant Colonel and Colonel, all by merit.

Sole paragraph The provisions of item I of this article do not apply to the Auxiliary Officers Board, created by Complementary Law No. 082 of March 18, 1993."

CHAPTER III

BASIC CONDITIONS

Art. 11: Entry into the career of PM Officer is made in the initial ranks, as considered in the specific legislation for each cadre, once the legal requirements have been met.

Sole paragraph. The hierarchical order in which PM Officers are placed in the initial ranks is the result of their classification in a course or competition.

Art. 12: No PM officer will be promoted on transfer to the paid reserve or retirement.

Art. 13: In order to be promoted on the basis of seniority or merit, it is essential that the PM officer is included in the Access List (AQ).

Art. 14: To join the Accession Board, the PM Officer must meet the following essential requirements, established for each rank:

I - Access conditions:

a) interstice;

b) physical fitness;

c) those peculiar to each post in the different cadres;

II - Professional Concept;

III - Moral Concept.

Sole paragraph. The regulations of this Law shall define and detail the conditions for access and the procedures for assessing professional and moral concepts.

Art. 15: A commissioned officer, when holding a military police position, or one considered to be of a military police nature, shall be eligible for promotion on any of the criteria, without prejudice to the number of competitors regularly stipulated.

Art. 16: PM Officers who feel they have been disadvantaged as a result of the composition of an Access Board, in their right to promotion, may appeal to the General Commander of the Corporation, as the last resort in the administrative sphere.

§ In order to submit an appeal, the PM Officer will have 15 (fifteen) calendar days from receipt of the official communication of the act which he considers to be prejudicial to him, or from knowledge, in the OPM in which he serves, of the official publication in this regard.

§ Paragraph 2. Appeals regarding the composition of the Access Board and promotion must be resolved within a maximum of 30 (thirty) days from the date of receipt.

Art. 17: The PM Officer will be compensated for the lapse, as long as his right to promotion is recognized, when:

a) - has a favorable outcome to the appeal;

b) - cease to be missing or lost;

c) - is acquitted by a final judgment or dismissed from the case to which he or she is being held;

d) - is justified by the Justification Board;

e) - has been harmed by a proven administrative error.

CHAPTER IV

PROCESSING OF PROMOTIONS

Art. 18: The act of promulgation shall be effected by decree of the Governor of the State of Santa Catarina.

§ Paragraph 1. The act of promotion to the initial rank in the career and the acts of promotion to that rank and to the first rank of Senior Officer shall entail the issuance of a letter of patent by the Governor of the State of Santa Catarina.

§ Paragraph 2. The promotion to other ranks shall be apostilled to the last rank issued.

Art. 19: In the different Boards, the vacancies to be considered for promotion will come from:

a) - promotion to higher rank;

b) - aggregation;

c) - transition to inactivity;

d) - dismissal;

e) - death;

f) - increase in staff.

§ Paragraph 1 Vacancies are considered open:

a) - on the date of signature of the act that promotes, adds, passes into inactivity or dismisses, unless another date is established in the act itself;

b) - on the official date of death;

c) - as provided by law, in the event of an increase in the number of staff.

§ Paragraph 2 - Each vacancy in a given post will lead to vacancies in the lower posts, and this sequence will be interrupted at the post where there is a surplus.

§ Paragraph 3. Vacancies resulting from "ex-officio" transfers to the paid reserve, already foreseen, up to and including the date of promotion, shall also be taken into account.

§ Paragraph 4 does not apply to a PM officer who, while attached, is promoted and remains in the same position.

LAW No. 6.703/85 (Art. 1) - (DO- 12.854 of 11/12/85)

Paragraph 5 is added to article 19 of Law No. 6.215 of February 10, 1983, to read as follows:

"Art. 19 ....

§ Paragraph 5 - Aggregations resulting from the application of article 94 of Law No. 6.218 of February 10, 1983 do not open vacancies for promotion purposes."

Art. 20: Promotions will be made annually, by seniority or merit, on January 31st, May 5th and August 25th.

LAW 13.569/05 (Art. 1) - (DO. 17.766 of 23/11/05)

The caput of art. 20 of Law no. 6.215, of February 10, 1983, shall come into force with the following wording:

"Art. 20: Promotions will be made annually, by seniority or merit, on January 31st, May 5th, August 11th and November 25th."

Sole paragraph. Seniority in rank shall be counted from the date of the act of promotion, with the exception of cases where non-computable time has been deducted in accordance with the Military Police Statute and post-mortem promotion, for bravery and to compensate for pretermination, when another date may be set.

Art. 21: Promotion by seniority in any cadre is made in the sequence of the respective seniority access cadre.

Art. 22: Promotion by merit is based on the merit-based access chart, in accordance with the regulations of this law.

Art. 23: The promotion for an act of bravery, under the terms of art. 7 of this Law, will be carried out by the Governor of the State, if practiced:

I - in support of Internal Defense and Territorial Defense, the Military Police is used as an Auxiliary Force, a reserve of the Army.

II - in the maintenance of public order.

§ Paragraph 1. The act of bravery, considered highly meritorious, is that which is determined in an investigation carried out by a Special Council appointed for this purpose by the Commanding General.

§ Paragraph 2. In the case of promotion for bravery, the requirements for promotion by another criterion established in this Law shall not apply.

§ Paragraph 3. The promoted officer shall be given the opportunity, where appropriate, to meet the conditions for access to the rank to which he has been promoted, in accordance with the regulations of this Law.

Art. 24: The "post-mortem" promotion is effective when the Officer dies in one of the following situations.

a) - in an action to maintain public order;

b) - as a result of injury received in the maintenance of public order, or illness, disease or infirmity contracted in this situation, or caused by it;

c) - as a result of an accident on duty, as defined by the Commanding General, or as a result of illness, disease or infirmity that has its efficient cause.

§ The officer will also be promoted if, at the time of his death, he met the conditions for access and was part of the group of those who were in the running for promotion by the criteria of seniority or merit.

§ Paragraph 2 The promotion resulting from any of the situations set out in letters "a", "b" and "c" of the heading of this article shall be independent of that provided for in Paragraph 1.

§ Paragraph 3. The cases of death due to illness, disease or infirmity referred to in this article will be proven by a certificate of origin, a health inquiry of origin, and the terms of the accident, hospital discharge, treatment papers in the wards and hospitals will be used as subsidiary means to clarify the situation.

§ Paragraph 4. In the event of the officer's death, the promotion for bravery excludes the "post-mortem" promotion that would result from the consequences of the act of bravery.

CHAPTER V

THE OFFICERS' PROMOTION COMMITTEE

Art. 25: The PM Officer Promotion Commission (CPOPM) is the body responsible for processing PM officer promotions.

Sole paragraph: the work of this body, which involves evaluating the merit of a PM Officer and the respective documentation, will be classified as confidential.

Art. 26: The PM Officers' Promotion Commission is permanent, made up of natural and permanent members and chaired by the General Commander of the Corporation.

§ Paragraph 1 - The Chief of Staff and the Director of Personnel of the Corporation are natural born members.

§ Paragraph 2 - Half of the ready Colonels of the Military Police and four (4) more Senior Military Police Officers, who are replaced annually, shall be effective members.

§ Paragraph 3: When filling vacancies for the rank of Colonel, the Commission for the Promotion of Military Officers (CPOPM) will be made up exclusively of all the ready-made Colonels of the Military Police.

§ Paragraph 4 - The CPOPM will be secretariat by a senior officer appointed by the Commanding General.

§ Paragraph 5 - The regulations of this Law shall define the duties and operation of the CPOPM.

CHAPTER VI

ACCESS PANELS

Art. 27 - Access Boards are lists of Officers from the different Boards organized by rank for promotion by seniority - Access Board by Seniority (QAA) and by merit (QAM), provided for in articles 5 and 6 of this Law.

§ Paragraph 1 - The Seniority Access List is the list of Officers eligible for access, placed in descending order of seniority.

§ Paragraph 2 The Access by Merit List is the list of Officers eligible for access and is the result of an assessment of the merit and quality required for promotion, which must take into account, in addition to other requirements

I - efficiency in the performance of positions and commissions, not their intrinsic nature or the length of time they have been held;

II - the potential for higher positions;

III - leadership skills, initiative and quick decision-making;

IV - the results of the regulatory courses held;

V - the Officer's prominence among his peers.

§ Paragraph 3. The seniority and merit access panels shall be organized for each date of promulgation in the manner established in the regulations of this Law.

Art. 28: Only officers who meet the conditions for access and fall within the quantitative seniority limits set out in the regulations of this law will be listed by the CPOPM for study for inclusion in the Access Ranks.

Sole paragraph. The percentage limits for promotion by seniority referred to in this article are intended to establish, by rank in the Boards, the ranks of the Officers competing to make up the Access Boards.

Art. 29: An officer may not be included on any Access Board when:

I - fails to meet the conditions required in Article 14(I);

II - is considered unqualified for provisional entry, at the discretion of the Commission for the Promotion of Officers, for presumably being unable to meet any of the requirements set out in article 14, paragraphs II and III;

LC N° 130/94 (Art.3) - (DO. 15.054 of 16/11/94)

... item II of Article 29 of Law No. 6.215 of February 10, 1983, shall read as follows:

Art. 29...

II - is convicted, for the duration of the main sentence, excluding the excess period of conditional suspension, if granted."

III - is arrested on remand, or in flagrante delicto, as long as the arrest has not been revoked;

IV - is subject to an ex-officio Justification Board;

V - is indicted in criminal proceedings, as long as the final judgment has not been passed;

VI - is sentenced, for the duration of the sentence, including in the case of conditional suspension of the sentence, and the time added to the original sentence for the purposes of its conditional suspension shall not be computed;

VII - is on leave to attend to a private interest;

VIII - is sentenced to suspension from the exercise of rank, office or function, as provided for in the Military Criminal Code, during the period of his suspension;

IX   - is considered missing;

X   - is considered lost;

XI - is considered deserted;

XII - is preventively arrested as a result of a military police investigation;

XIII- is in debt with the Public Treasury, by scope.

LC N° 130/94 (Art.15) - (DO. 15.054 of 16/11/94)

"Subsections IV, V, XII and XIII of Article 29 of Law No. 6.215 of February 10, 1983 are hereby repealed."

§ Paragraph 1 - Officers who fall foul of item II of this article shall be subject to an ex-officio Council of Justification."

§ Paragraph 2 - Upon receipt of the report of the Council of Justification, set up in accordance with the previous paragraph, the Governor of the state, in his decision, if applicable, will consider the officer to be unqualified for access on a definitive basis, in accordance with the specific legislation.

§ Paragraph 3. An officer who incurs one of the circumstances set out in this article, or who also incurs one of the circumstances set out in this article, shall be excluded from any Access Board:

a) - is unduly included in it;

b) - has died;

c) - go into inactivity.

Art. 30 An officer who joins or is joined shall be excluded from or may not be included in the merit-based access roster that has already been organized:

I - due to leave for treatment of a family member's health, for a period equal to or greater than 6 (six) continuous months;

II - by virtue of being in temporary, non-elective civilian public office or function, including Indirect Administration and Foundations established by the State;

III - for having entered the service of a federal, state or municipal government to perform a civilian function.

Sole paragraph To be eligible for inclusion or reinclusion in the merit-based access cadre, the officer covered by this article must rejoin the Corps at least 90 days before the date of promotion.

Art. 31 An officer who fails to appear three times, consecutively or not, on a merit-based access board, if a more modern officer participated in each board, shall be considered ineligible for promotion to the next rank on the merit-based criterion.

Paragraph 1: A lieutenant colonel who appears at the head of the list three (3) consecutive times for promotion on merit may not be passed over.

Art. 32 Officers who have been promoted unduly will become surplus to requirements.

Paragraph 1: This officer shall count seniority and receive the number that corresponds to him in the hierarchical scale, when the vacancy to be filled corresponds to the criterion by which he should be promoted, provided that he meets the requirements for promotion.

Art. 33 Officers are considered to be unqualified for access on a permanent basis only when they are in the situation provided for in § 2 of art. 29 of this Law.

CHAPTER VII

FINAL AND TRANSITIONAL PROVISIONS

Art. 34 The provisions of this Law shall apply to PM officer aspirants, as far as they are concerned.

Art. 35 The Executive Branch is hereby authorized to regulate this Law within 60 (sixty) days of its publication.

Art. 36 Officers in the Health Service who, on the date of approval of this Law, have completed 8 (eight) or more years of service in the rank of Major or Captain in the said Service, will be promoted to the next rank, by seniority, regardless of whether there are any vacancies after completing 10 years of effective service.

Art. 37 This law shall enter into force on the date of its publication.

Art. 38 Law No. 4.558 of January 1971 and other provisions to the contrary are hereby repealed.

Government Palace in Florianopolis, February 10, 1983

HENRIQUE HELION VELHO DE CORDOVA

State Governor

REFERENCES

ANDRADE, Rui Otavio Bernardes de; AMBONI, Nerio. **Estrategias de gestao**: processos e funpoes do administrador. Rio de Janeiro: Elsevier, 2010.

CHIAVENATO, Idalberto. **Managing with people**: transforming the executive into an excellent people manager. Rio de Janeiro: Elsevier, 2005.

CHIAVENATO. Idalberto. **People management**. 3. ed. Rio de Janeiro: Elsevier, 2010.

GIRARDI, Dante et al. People management in entrepreneurial organizations. In: LAPOLLI, Edis Mafra et al. (org.). **Gestao de pessoas em Organizapoes Empreendedoras**. Florianopolis: Pandion, 2009, p. 2141.

LAPOLLI, Juliana; SILVA, Gleice Schurhaus da; SANTO, Rosana Goulart do Espirito. The selection process in entrepreneurial organizations. In: LAPOLLI, Edis Mafra et al. (org.) **Gestao de pessoas em Organizapoes Empreendedoras**. Florianopolis: Pandion, 2009, p. 91-111.

LUCENA, Maria Diva da Salete. **Planning human resources**. Sao Paulo: Atlas, 1999.

MACHADO, Edson Valdir; MELCHERT, Gisele Schmidt; MAKUFKA, Merilin. NEWTON QUADROS: a case of management today. In: LAPOLLI, Juliana; LAPOLLI, Edis Mafra (org.) **Gestao de pessoas na actualidade**: investindo no capital humano. Florianopolis: Pandion, 2011, p. 185-199.

MARRAS, Jean Pierre. **Human resources management**: from operational to strategic. 14. ed. Sao Paulo: Saraiva, 2011.

MICHAELIS. Modern dictionary (online). Available at: <http://michaelis.uol.com.br/moderno/portugues/index.php?lingua=portugues-portugues&palavra=gest%E3o>. Accessed on: Aug. 31, 2014.

RABAGLIO, Maria Odete. **Selection by competence**. Sao Paulo: Educator, 2001.

REIS, Valeria dos. **The selection interview with a focus on behavioral competencies**. Rio de Janeiro: Qualitymark, 2003.

RESENDE, Enio. **The book of competencies**: Developing competencies: The best self-help for individuals, organizations and society. 2. ed. Rio de Janeiro: Qualitymark, 2003.

RESENDE, Enio. **Remuneration and career based on competencies and skills**. Rio de Janeiro: Qualitymark, 2002.

RUANO, Alessandra Martinewski. **Competency-based management**: a perspective for the consolidation of strategic human resources management. Rio de Janeiro: Qualitymark, 2003.

SANTA CATARINA (State). State Secretariat for Public Security. Santa Catarina Military Police. **Command Plan**: Military Police of Santa Catarina. Florianopolis: PMSC, 2013.

SANTA CATARINA (State). State Secretariat for Public Security. Military Police of Santa Catarina. **Strategic Plan**: Santa Catarina Military Police. 3.ed. Florianopolis: PMSC, 2015.

SANTA CATARINA (State). Decree No. 19.236, of March 14, 1983a. Regulates the Law on the Promotion of Officers in the State Military Police. Available at: <http://www.pge.sc.gov.br/index.php/legislacao-estadual- pge>. Accessed on: August 3, 2014.

SANTA CATARINA (State). Law No. 6.215, of February 10, 1983b. Provides for the Promotion of State Military Police Officers, and other measures. Disponivel em: <http://200.192.66.20/alesc/docs/1983/6218_1983_lei.doc>. Accessed on: September 10, 2014.

SANTA CATARINA (State). Law No. 6.218, of February 10, 1983c. Provides for the Statute of the Military Police of the State of Santa Catarina, and other measures. Disponivel em: <http://200.192.66.20/alesc/docs/1983/6218_1983_lei.doc>. Accessed on: September 10, 2014.

SNELL, Scott; BOHLANDER, George. **Human resources management.** Translated by Maria Lucia G. L. Rosa and Solange Aparecida Visconti. Sao Paulo: Cengage Learning, 2010.